World Book, Inc.
180 North LaSalle Street
Suite 900
Chicago, Illinois 60601
USA

For information about other "True or False?" titles, as
well as other World Book print and digital publications,
please go to www.worldbook.com.

For information about other World Book publications,
call 1-800-WORLDBK (967-5325).

For information about sales to schools and libraries,
call 1-800-975-3250 (United States) or 1-800-837-5365
(Canada).

Library of Congress Cataloging-in-Publication Data for
this volume has been applied for.

True or False?
ISBN: 978-0-7166-3725-7 (set, hc.)

Mammals
ISBN: 978-0-7166-3730-1 (hc.)

Also available as:
ISBN: 978-0-7166-3740-0 (e-book)

Printed in China by Shenzhen Wing King Tong Paper
Products Co., Ltd., Shenzhen, Guangdong
1st printing July 2018

Staff

Executive Committee

President
Jim O'Rourke

Vice President and
Editor in Chief
Paul A. Kobasa

Vice President, Finance
Donald D. Keller

Vice President, Marketing
Jean Lin

Vice President, International
Maksim Rutenberg

Vice President, Technology
Jason Dole

Director, Human Resources
Bev Ecker

Editorial

Director, New Print
Tom Evans

Writers
Grace Guibert
Mellonee Carrigan

Editor
Will Adams

Librarian
S. Thomas Richardson

Manager, Contracts and
Compliance
(Rights and Permissions)
Loranne K. Shields

Manager, Indexing Services
David Pofelski

Digital

Director, Digital Product
Development
Erika Meller

Digital Product Manager
Jonathan Wills

Manufacturing/Production

Manufacturing Manager
Anne Fritzinger

Production Specialist
Curley Hunter

Proofreader
Nathalie Strassheim

Graphics and Design

Senior Art Director
Tom Evans

Senior Visual
Communications Designer
Melanie Bender

Senior Designer
Isaiah Sheppard

Media Editor
Rosalia Bledsoe

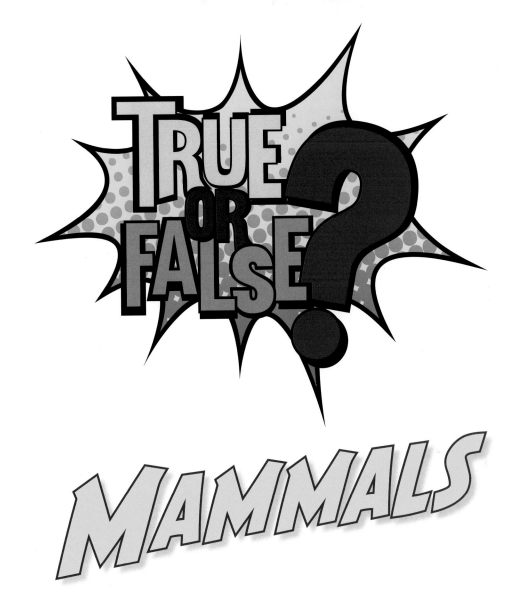

MAMMALS

WORLD
BOOK

www.worldbook.com

Dogs are related to bats, dolphins, and kangaroos.

5

**All of these animals are *mammals.*
Mammals are animals that feed their young
on the mother's milk. They are the only
animals with true hair. (Bees look fuzzy,
for instance, but their fuzz isn't hair.)**

Mammals are *warm-blooded*. This means that a mammal's body temperature usually stays the same. Mammal brains are larger and more complex than the brains of other animals.

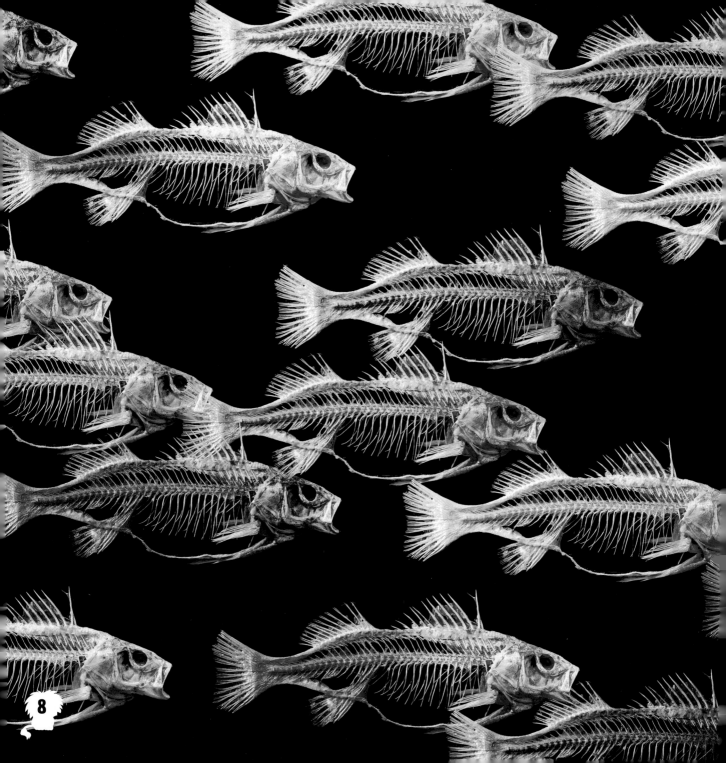

Fish, birds, snakes, and frogs are mammals because they have backbones.

All mammals have backbones, but not all animals with backbones are mammals. An animal with a backbone is called a *vertebrate* (VUR tuh brayte).

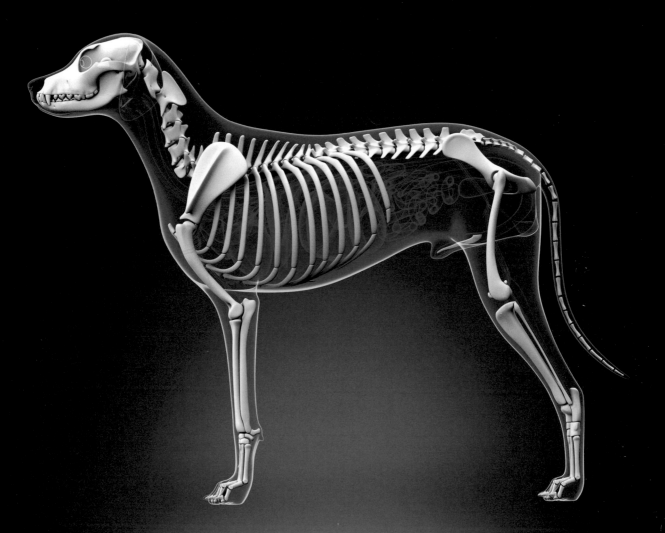

Mammals are one *class*, or group, of vertebrates. Other classes include fish, birds, reptiles (like alligators, snakes, and lizards), and amphibians (like salamanders, frogs, and toads).

TRUE OR FALSE?

Mammals only live on land.

13

FALSE!

Mammals live almost everywhere.
Seals and whales are two of the many
mammals that swim in the oceans.

But all mammals need to breathe air. Underwater mammals, like whales, come to the surface of the water to breathe air.

Some mammals lay eggs.

16

Most mammals give birth to live babies. But two kinds of mammals lay eggs! They are called the duck-billed platypus *(PLAT uh puhs)* and the echidna *(ih KIHD nuh)*.

TRUE OR FALSE?

Mammals cannot fly.

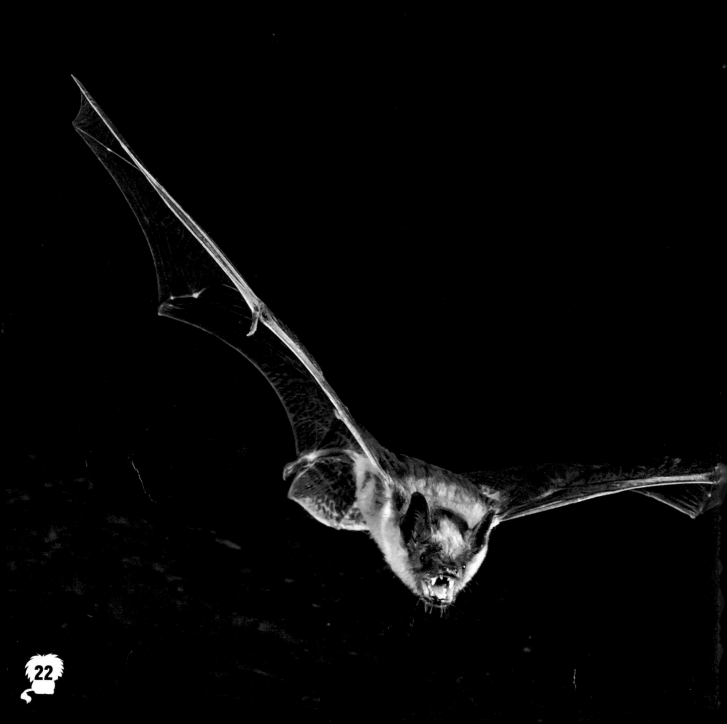

Some mammals can fly: bats!
Flying squirrels and flying possums are
also mammals. But these two kinds of
animals cannot truly fly — they just glide
through the air for short periods of time.

Sloths turn green in the rainy season.

24

A sloth's gray or brown fur turns green from the algae *(AL gee)* that grow in it during the rainy season. Algae are tiny living things. The sloth's green coat helps it blend into the rain forest trees where it lives. The color makes it hard for predators, like birds of prey and big cats, to see the sloths.

Gorillas burp to show happiness.

True! Gorillas are huge apes that look fierce. But they are friendly animals! They seem to need friends and like attention from other gorillas. Instead of laughing, gorillas burp when they are happy!

Camels keep water in their humps.

Camels' humps hold fat. The camel can use
this fat for energy when food and water
are hard to find. A camel can go for days
or even months without drinking!

34

35

TRUE OR FALSE?

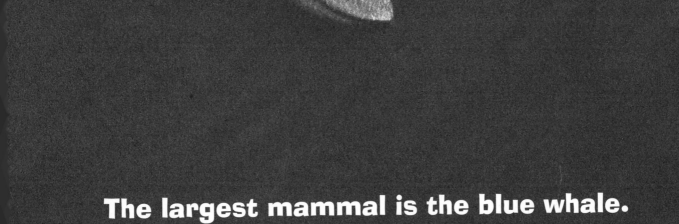

The largest mammal is the blue whale.

TRUE!

38

The blue whale is also the largest animal of any kind to ever live on Earth—bigger than even the biggest dinosaurs! A blue whale can grow to be 100 feet (30 meters) long. It can weigh more than 300,000 pounds (140,000 kilograms).

Cheetahs, lions, and tigers all run
at about the same speed.

Cheetahs are the fastest land animals in the world. Cheetahs can run 50 to 70 miles (80 to 110 kilometers) per hour. That's as fast as a car traveling on a highway! Lions and tigers are fast, too. But they can't keep up with the cheetah!

Mice love cheese.

Mice have an excellent sense of smell.
They don't like stinky things! Mice might
eat cheese sometimes, but they like
fruits, breads, and crackers much more.
Mice can use their sharp teeth to chew
into bags and boxes of food!

46

Spotted skunks can do gymnastics.

48

TRUE!

Spotted skunks do handstands before they spray! Skunks use their smelly spray to keep other animals away. The spotted skunk's flashy handstand warns its enemies to back off.

50

51

TRUE OR FALSE?

Bulls are attracted to the color red.

FALSE!

In bullfights in such countries as Spain and Portugal, the matador (bullfighter) often waves a red cape at the bull. But bulls are color blind! The movement of the cape catches their eye. They would be just as drawn to a cape of another color.

**The rhinoceros is a close relative
of the hippopotamus.**

57

The rhinoceros and hippopotamus
have a similar body shape, but the
rhinoceros is more closely related to
the horse. The hippopotamus is a
relative of pigs, camels, and cows.

59

TRUE OR FALSE?

Kangaroos are *marsupials (mahr SOO pee uhlz)*. Baby marsupials grow in a pouch on their mother's belly.

61

TRUE!

Marsupial babies are tiny and helpless when first born. They need to keep growing inside their mothers' pouches before they can move around on their own. Kangaroo babies are only about 1 inch (2.5 centimeters) long when they are born! Koalas and opossums are other types of marsupials.

63

Giraffes can lick their ears.

Giraffes use their long tongues to pull leaves from tree branches to eat. But giraffe tongues are long enough to touch their ears, too! Giraffes' tongues are about 18 inches (46 centimeters) long—sometimes even longer.

Opossums hang by their tails from tree branches when they sleep.

69

Opossums spend most of their time on the ground, not in trees. Opossums might climb into trees to find food or hide from predators. Their long tails help opossums balance when they climb.

A tiger's skin is striped.

Tigers have striped skin to match their striped fur! Just like no two people have the same fingerprints, no two tigers have the same stripe pattern.

An elephant never forgets.

Elephants have great memories. They are especially good at remembering faces. Elephants remember other elephants that they met years and years ago! Elephants' sharp memories help them stay safe from strangers.

TRUE OR FALSE?

Bats are blind.

FALSE!

Some people think bats are blind. Most bats are color blind, but all bats can see and many have excellent vision. Bats also have strong senses of smell and hearing. Many bats sense their surroundings using *echolocation.* In echolocation, an animal learns about its surroundings from echoes of sounds it makes.

83

Koalas sleep for most of the day.

85

Koalas sleep longer than any other animal. Koalas sleep between 18 and 22 hours every day!

Mammals are not very
smart animals.

88

Some of the smartest animals on Earth are mammals. Humans are mammals! Apes can learn to speak to humans through sign language. Dolphins have their own ways of speaking to each other. Mammals are very smart!

DID YOU KNOW...

!!!!

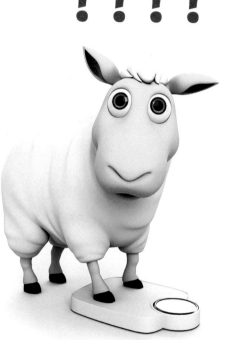

Blue whales are the loudest animal. Their whale calls can be heard from hundreds of miles away!

Most cats don't like water. But **tigers** love it! They swim to cool off.

Sheep have **four stomachs.**

Chimpanzees hug
each other to
show they care.

Giant pandas have giant appetites.
They eat up to
85 pounds
(39 kilograms) of bamboo shoots
every day!

There are
more than
5,000 species
(types) of
mammals.

Index

Acknowledgments

Cover: © Chereliss/Shutterstock; © Hogan Imaging/Shutterstock; © Dmitry Natashin, Shutterstock

4-21   © Shutterstock

22-23   © Frank Hildebrand, iStockphoto

25-35   © Shutterstock

36-37   © Mark Carwardine, Getty Images

38-53   © Shutterstock

54   © Syldavia/iStockphoto

57-93   © Shutterstock